She
Persisted

....

MARIA TALLCHIEF

....

— INSPIRED BY —

She Persisted

by Chelsea Clinton & Alexandra Boiger

· ·

MARIA TALLCHIEF

· ·

Written by
Christine Day

Interior illustrations by
Gillian Flint

PHILOMEL

PHILOMEL BOOKS
An imprint of Penguin Random House LLC, New York

First published in the United States of America by Philomel Books,
an imprint of Penguin Random House LLC, 2021

Visit us online at penguinrandomhouse.com.

Library of Congress Cataloging-in-Publication Data is available.

Printed in the United States of America

HC ISBN 9780593115800
10 9 8 7 6 5 4 3 2 1
PB ISBN 9780593115817
10 9 8 7 6 5 4 3 2 1

WRZL

Edited by Jill Santopolo.
Design by Ellice M. Lee.
Text set in LTC Kennerley.

∽ *For* ∾
the Osage Nation,
for Maria's living relatives,
and in honor of
Indigenous kids everywhere.

She
Persisted

....

Dear Reader,

As Sally Ride and Marian Wright Edelman both powerfully said, "You can't be what you can't see." When Sally said that, she meant that it was hard to dream of being an astronaut, like she was, or a doctor or an athlete or anything at all if you didn't see someone like you who already had lived that dream. She especially was talking about seeing women in jobs that historically were held by men.

I wrote the first *She Persisted* and the books that came after it because I wanted young girls—and children of all genders—to see women who worked hard to live their dreams. And I wanted all of us to see examples of persistence in the face of different challenges to help inspire us in our own lives.

I'm so thrilled now to partner with a sisterhood of writers to bring longer, more in-depth versions of these stories of women's persistence and achievement to readers. I hope you enjoy these chapter books as much as I do and find them inspiring and empowering.

And remember: If anyone ever tells you no, if anyone ever says your voice isn't important or your dreams are too big, remember these women. They persisted and so should you.

Warmly,

Chelsea Clinton

MARIA
TALLCHIEF

TABLE OF CONTENTS

....

CHAPTER I

𐓏𐒰𐓓𐒰𐓓𐒷 | *Osage*

When Elizabeth Marie Tall Chief was born, there were few American ballet stars. She would become one of the first. And to this day, she remains one of the most famous and celebrated dancers in history.

We know her as Maria Tallchief. Growing up, she was nicknamed Betty.

Betty was born in Fairfax, Oklahoma, on January 24, 1925. Her father, Alexander, was a citizen of the Osage Nation. Her mother, Ruth, was a white woman from Oxford, Kansas. Her parents met when Ruth went to Fairfax to visit her sister, who worked as a cook and housekeeper in Alexander's mother's home. At the time, it was common for Osage people to live in mansions. In the 1920s, the Osage tribal members were among the wealthiest people in the world.

When Ruth and Alexander initially met, he was a handsome widower, which meant he'd been married but his spouse had passed away. He had three children from his first marriage, and after he and Ruth were married, they had three more children together. The first was Betty's brother, Jerry. Betty came next, and was closely followed by her sister, Marjorie.

Ruth wanted her daughters to do ballet,

because she loved the arts but couldn't afford to attend lessons when she was a little girl. And so, Betty took her first ballet lesson when she was three years old. Throughout her childhood, she spent most of her time doing schoolwork—and learning how to dance.

As the family grew, Alexander's eldest children moved in with their grandmother, Eliza Tall Chief. Eliza was very involved in the raising of her grandchildren, including Betty, and she helped them stay connected to their Osage culture.

The Osage Nation has a long and complicated history. By the time Betty was born, the Osages had already endured many hardships.

In the 1800s, the Osages and other Native Nations suffered in the area known as Indian Territory, which got smaller and smaller until it made up only most of what is now the state of Oklahoma. Diseases spread through their communities. Fences were built to separate the people from the roaming buffalo, a food Native Nations ate to stay strong.

Then, in 1871, the Osage Nation bought their own reservation in northeastern Oklahoma. Nobody knew it yet, but the land they reserved for themselves was filled with oil. When they found it, the Osage leaders made sure it was shared equally by all members of the tribe—and people paid a lot of money for that oil!

This is how the Osages became so wealthy.

However, their riches didn't solve everything. The Osage Nation and the US government still had conflicts. For many years, the US government wanted Natives to "assimilate" into American society. This meant that Native people were expected to speak only English, change religions, and forget their cultures. Because of this, many Osage children were sent to boarding schools, and Osage elders could only share their histories and traditions in secret.

As a young girl, Betty learned some of these secrets. Alexander and Eliza took the family to powwows held in remote corners of the Osage reservation. If they had been caught, they could

have gotten in trouble. At the time, Native American ceremonies and gatherings were illegal. (And they would remain illegal until Congress passed the American Indian Religious Freedom Act in 1978, when Betty was fifty-three years old!)

But the family went, even though there were risks. It was important for Betty and her siblings to learn about their tribe's culture, their values, and their history.

Betty never forgot the rhythm of those pow-wow songs.

When Betty was eight years old, her brother, Jerry, went to military school. Shortly after that, Alexander, Ruth, Betty, and Marjorie moved to California.

It was a bittersweet time. Betty loved her house in Fairfax. She loved the big front yard, with its old swing and its blooming garden. She loved the horse pastures and the rolling green lands that surrounded her home.

Nevertheless, her family moved further west.

....

ꙆO7ΛÞꙆ | *Student*

When they reached California, Betty felt hypnotized by the bright, endless orange groves. And the Pacific Ocean seemed to be everywhere, lurking beyond curves in the road, hiding between gaps in the trees. After the ponds and creeks of Oklahoma, Betty was terrified by the size of the ocean.

The Tall Chief family settled in Beverly Hills. Throughout their first few years in Los

Angeles, Betty and Marjorie attended Ernest Belcher's dance school.

Betty learned a lot from Ernest Belcher. In addition to classical ballet training, she was exposed to tap dancing, acrobatics, and Spanish dancing. All of her lessons were challenging, but the acrobatics were especially difficult. Betty complained about them so much, her mother eventually let her stop taking them. (However, when Betty grew up, she was grateful for her background in acrobatics. Everything she learned there was put to good use in her professional dance career.)

But as she continued to grow older, Betty felt unchallenged in her regular schooling. Back in Fairfax, Betty had skipped ahead two grades in school. In Los Angeles, she was placed in advanced

programs at her age level, but she continued to test and perform above her classmates. After finishing her work, she would often wander around the schoolyard by herself.

Los Angeles has always been a home to Native people. Long before the Spanish missionaries arrived, the area known as Los Angeles was called Tovaangar. *Tovaangar* is a word that means "the world" in the Tongva language, and it referenced the many villages the ancestors of the Gabrieliño-Tongvas lived in. The Tatavium, the Chumash, the Serrano, the Cahuilla, and the Luiseño tribal communities also had their homes in Southern California. For thousands of years, these groups of people—among others—lived and thrived there.

But despite these histories and the Native people who were still living in California, Betty often felt alone and different. She was a shy, quiet girl who struggled to make friends. She was also bullied by her classmates in school. They made "war whoops" whenever they saw her. They asked her why she didn't wear feathers in her hair. They made racist, hurtful comments about her father. And they made fun of her last name, pretending to be confused by whether it was *Tall* or *Chief.*

Betty changed the spelling of her name into one word: *Tallchief,* instead of *Tall Chief.* Everything in her school was organized in alphabetical order, and she wanted to avoid confusion.

She also probably hoped that the bullying would stop altogether.

． ． ．

When Betty was twelve years old, she and Marjorie transferred to a new ballet studio. This school was run by a woman named Madame Nijinska, who was a graduate of the Imperial Theatre School in St. Petersburg, Russia. In her youth, she had performed on stages all across Europe. She was also a choreographer, which meant she created dance routines and ballets for practices and performances.

She was an impressive woman and a strict teacher. Madame Nijinska didn't speak much English; dance was the common language between her and her students. She communicated by demonstrating movements across the floor, while her students followed her footwork.

Madame Nijinska inspired Betty. She had liked ballet before, but in this new studio, Betty fell in love with it. She was still only twelve years old, but suddenly, she knew this was what she wanted to do for the rest of her life.

In Madame Nijinska's pointe classes, Betty and her classmates repeated the same steps over and over, learning how to balance. Madame Nijinska would adjust their arms and elbows so that each position looked elegant. And as the dance students practiced their soaring jumps and spins, Madame Nijinska taught them to tense their stomach muscles for more control.

As Betty continued to work hard as a dance student, she started to carry herself like a ballerina outside of the studio. She became more aware of her posture. Whenever she went to

bed, she imagined herself sleeping like a ballerina.
Whenever she stood in place, she stood as if she
were under a spotlight. She became dedicated to
her dance education.

She lived and breathed the art of ballet.

ᖴᐱᒉᑎ ᐅᐱᒧᐱᒪᐊ | *First Performance*

When Betty was fifteen years old, Madame Nijinska staged a grand ballet production at the Hollywood Bowl. Betty was thrilled by the opportunity. She believed this moment would be her big break as a dancer, and would be the first of many lead roles for her. She had worked hard for three years in Madame Nijinska's studio. She had become one of the school's top students.

But when Madame Nijinska announced the

cast of dancers, Betty wasn't chosen for one of the lead roles. Instead, she was placed in the corps—the group of background dancers in a ballet. Betty didn't understand why her teacher had overlooked her.

During the rehearsals, Betty no longer felt motivated to do her best. She felt bitter and jealous of the girls in the leading roles. She was miserable. She rehearsed her role in the corps without putting any emotion or real effort into what she was doing.

Ruth told her daughter to snap out of it. She said, "You have to show that you want to dance with all your heart, Betty, even in the corps. You shouldn't just expect a role to be handed to you."

Betty would never forget this lesson. Encouraged by her mother's words, she persisted. Betty returned to the rehearsals and worked harder than ever. She treated each practice session as if it were a real performance.

Madame Nijinska noticed. And she recast Betty in one of the lead roles.

The Hollywood Bowl is an enormous outdoor theater. Located between rolling, golden-brown hills dotted with greenery, it has hosted countless famous performances. And after all her hard work, Betty still believed that this was going to be her big moment.

But on the day of the ballet production, she was late.

Since this was her first major performance, Betty didn't know that dancers were supposed to arrive and prepare two hours before showtime. Unlike the other ballerinas, she made it to the

Hollywood Bowl with only fifteen minutes to spare.

Flustered by her lateness, and giddy with nerves, Betty hurried through her warm-ups. She tied the ribbons of her pointe shoes quickly. She went onstage, her heart hammering in her chest.

And as soon as she started dancing, she slipped.

She felt shaken and embarrassed by her mistake. She worried that she had let her teacher

and her family down. After so many flawless rehearsals, it seemed unfair that this was how her debut performance had begun.

Nevertheless, the show must go on.

Once she recovered, she attempted to perform as Madame Nijinska had taught her. And she tried not to let herself get flustered again, no matter what happened before she went onstage.

As the end of her high school years approached, Betty started to look for work as a professional dancer. Since she lived in Los Angeles, most of the jobs available were in movie musicals. And so, Betty went to Hollywood and was cast as a background dancer in the movie *Presenting Lily Mars* (1943). It was a fun experience. Betty enjoyed being on the set. She felt inspired by the hardworking actresses around her. And her parents were proud of her.

But as filming ended, Betty realized she didn't want to perform in movie musicals for the rest of her career. The routines weren't very challenging. The dancing roles were mostly small. Betty missed the discipline and fulfillment of ballet dancing.

If she wanted to keep growing as a dancer, and especially as a ballerina, Betty needed to leave Los Angeles.

When Betty was seventeen years old, she traveled to the traditional Lenape territory known as New York City. She went there to audition for the Ballet Russe de Monte Carlo, a famous ballet company that frequently toured the world. It was a big risk, and she was nervous about moving to another new city while her parents and sister stayed behind in California. But she was determined to find work as a professional ballet dancer.

Betty packed a giant suitcase and bid farewell to her family at the train terminal.

She was on her way.

....

ᏙᎭᏓᏏᏞᎠ | *Rising Star*

Soon after she arrived in New York City, Betty joined the Ballet Russe de Monte Carlo as an apprentice. This means that she was a beginner in the world of professional ballet. At first, they wouldn't let her audition. But when the company realized that some of their dancers weren't allowed to travel outside of the United States because they were born in countries that were fighting the US during World War II, Betty got her chance. She traveled with the company for their Canadian tour in 1942, and the program changed constantly. The dancers would learn new routines during the day, then perform them each night. It was a demanding schedule, but Betty was a fast learner and a confident dancer.

This was the type of challenge she'd been hoping for.

After the Canadian tour ended, Betty was offered a permanent position with the company. She happily accepted the job and continued to work hard in each role she was given.

However, when her boss asked her to change her last name, she refused. He'd suggested "Tallchieva," because it sounded Russian and most well-known ballerinas at the time came from Russia. But Betty loved her name. It connected her to her family and to her Osage identity. She didn't want to give up this important part of herself.

Then, one afternoon, a choreographer named Agnes de Mille found Betty alone in the studio. Betty was still practicing her routine after the company's rehearsals had ended for the day and everyone else had gone home. Miss de Mille was impressed by her, and she offered Betty some advice:

"There are so many Bettys and Elizabeths in ballet. If I were you, I'd think about changing my name. Why don't you use your middle name alone and call yourself Maria? You could be Maria Tallchief."

Betty liked this idea, so she adopted it for the stage.

And as Maria Tallchief, she continued to rise.

Over the next few years, Maria traveled and performed with the Ballet Russe de Monte Carlo. She was promoted from the corps de ballet to the rank of soloist. She was given many kinds of roles, and continued to learn and grow throughout her time with the company.

Then, in 1948, the New York City Ballet was born, and Maria joined the new company. The New York City Ballet struggled at first. Their ticket sales were low. Their seasons were short. Their early reviews were generally negative.

And so, Maria also joined the American Ballet Theatre, and spent a year going back and forth between the two companies. With the American Ballet Theatre, she performed classic roles such as the Swan Queen in *Swan Lake*. With the New York City Ballet, she premiered as the lead in new ballets such as *Orpheus*, choreographed by George Balanchine. Balanchine was the company's founder and artistic director, and he was also Maria's first husband. Their marriage only lasted a few years, but they remained lifelong friends and colleagues.

On November 27, 1949, Maria starred in the New York City Ballet's opening night of *Firebird*.

All day long, Maria worried that the show would be a disaster. She and her dance partner had fumbled during the rehearsal, and her Firebird costume wasn't ready until about ten minutes before the performance. She hurried to put it on, and she pinned the feathered crown in place. And then—moments before the curtain lifted—she realized she hadn't rehearsed with the crown at all. She worried that it might fall off, but there was nothing she could do about it.

Maria took a deep breath and jumped out onto the stage.

Once she was in the spotlight, Maria's worries went away. The routine was one of the most difficult she had ever performed, but she remembered her mother's advice from long ago, and danced with all her heart. She had worked so hard. She had earned this role. And as she moved across the stage, she truly felt like a magical, mythical firebird.

When the ballet ended, the audience erupted in applause. They roared and cheered and chanted her name, "Tallchief! Tallchief! Tallchief!" Over and over, they clapped and celebrated and called for an encore: "Tallchief! Tallchief! Tallchief!"

Maria was stunned. She couldn't believe it.

Their cheers reminded her of a football stadium after a touchdown. In all her years performing on the world's stages, Maria had never heard anything like it in a ballet theater before.

CHAPTER 5

ᐱᒉᓂᔎᐱ | *Breaking Barriers*

For many years, Maria performed with the New York City Ballet. She traveled in the company's international tours. After dancing in other countries, she would return to New York, where she worked long, exhausting days. George Balanchine created new roles for her, and whole ballets around her, and she was onstage almost every night. She often received standing ovations and thunderous applause for her performances.

She had never worked harder. But she had also never been happier.

Maria was officially a star. She received glowing reviews in major newspapers and magazines. *Dance Magazine*, *Mademoiselle*, and *The New York Times* published articles about her. She was named Woman of the Year by the Washington Press Club. Movie stars and celebrities requested backstage passes at the ballet just to meet Maria. Famous writers composed poetry inspired by her dancing. Photographers also captured her in their work. She had countless devoted fans.

Even though she was grateful for their generosity and kindness, Maria tried to ignore the endless praise. She sometimes felt overwhelmed by all the attention and admiration. And she believed that critics and audiences could be a distraction. She cared more about challenging herself and dancing with her heart than pleasing the people who watched her.

Throughout her career, she inspired many iconic roles, including the Sugar Plum Fairy in Balanchine's *The Nutcracker*. She mostly danced with the New York City Ballet, but occasionally took seasons off to travel with the Ballet Russe de Monte Carlo and to perform principal roles with the American Ballet Theatre. She also played the role of Anna Pavlova in the classic film *Million Dollar Mermaid* (1952). She appeared as a guest artist with the Chicago Opera Ballet, the San Francisco Ballet, the Royal Danish Ballet, and the Hamburg Ballet. She was the first American ballerina to ever perform at the Bolshoi Theatre in

Russia, as well as the Paris Opera Ballet in France. When Maria was forty years old, she retired from dancing professionally.

Maria settled in Chicago, where she became a ballet teacher and artistic director and married again. She also became a mother when her daughter, Elise, was born on a snowy January day in 1959. Maria founded the School of the Lyric Opera in 1974, and launched the Chicago City Ballet with her sister, Marjorie, in 1980. (Marjorie had also built an impressive career as a dancer, achieving international fame at the Paris Opera Ballet.)

All her life, Maria strongly believed in the importance of securing and preserving Native American rights and traditions. During her retirement, she decided to get even more involved with Native American activism. She volunteered on the leadership board of an organization called Americans for Indian Opportunity. She often spoke to Native groups and children about the arts, and she lectured in schools and universities. She also joined the fundraising committee for the National Museum of the American Indian at the Smithsonian Institution.

Later in her life, Maria developed arthritis. Despite the condition, which made her joints hurt, she continued to work hard. She maintained a steady routine in Chicago by rising at 5 a.m. each day, and staying active and engaged with the ballet world, her dance students, and her daughter and grandchildren. She treated her arthritis with herbs and Tylenol.

In 1987, when Maria was sixty-two years old, her pharmacist asked if her long dance career had

been worth all the aches and pains.

"Oh yes. It was," she answered. "It certainly was."

Maria worked hard and dreamed big, not only for herself but for her family, her people, and the world she lived in. She was a dancer, a teacher, an artistic director, a mother and grandmother, an advocate for the arts, and a fighter for Native American rights.

She was an inspiration.

ᎣᏏᎳᎦ ᏅᏜᎳ | *A Legacy*

Elizabeth Marie Tall Chief died on April 11, 2013, in Chicago, Illinois. She was eighty-eight years old. She was survived by her sister, Marjorie; her daughter, Elise; and her two grandchildren, Alexandra and Stephen.

She was inducted into the National Women's Hall of Fame, as well as the National Native American's Hall of Fame. She received a Kennedy Center Honor from President Bill Clinton for

her contribution to the arts, as well as the
National Medal of the Arts. These are two of
the highest honors that any American artist—
whether a musician, writer, actor, or dancer—

can hope to achieve, and she earned them both. When she received her Kennedy Center Honor, she was the only woman among the honorees. She was also the only dancer.

Maria Tallchief is still widely considered to be one of the greatest and most influential ballerinas in history. At the height of her career, she was the highest-paid dancer in the world. She took risks and broke barriers. She was the first American to dance on many of the world's stages. She was also the first American to earn the title of prima ballerina, which is the highest possible rank for a dancer in a ballet company.

And to this day, *The Nutcracker*—a ballet she made famous through her role as the Sugar Plum Fairy—remains the most popular ballet in America. It is an annual ballet box office hit and a beloved holiday tradition for many families.

Many dance organizations in Oklahoma continue to honor Maria Tallchief's legacy. The Maria Tallchief Endowed Scholarship was created by the University of Oklahoma to provide their college-level dance students with financial assistance. The Dance Maker Academy, which is located on the Osage reservation, shares the joys of a dance education with all members of the community, regardless of age or experience. And the Osage Ballet produced a ballet called *Wahzhazhe*, a significant production that shares four hundred years of Osage history through the art of ballet. Like Maria, the Osage Ballet has traveled widely to share their story and their artistry with the world. In 2013, they were invited to the Smithsonian's National Museum of the

American Indian, where they performed to sold-
out audiences. In 2013, they were invited to the
Smithsonian's National Museum of the American
Indian, where there are statues honoring the

Tallchief sisters. The Osage Ballet performed there to sold-out audiences.

In addition to all of these organizations and awards, Maria also inspired thousands of young people. From the dance students she worked with at the School of the Lyric Opera, to the girls who pinned her magazine photos to the walls in their bedrooms, to the kids who learned from her lectures, Maria shared her gifts and knowledge with them all.

Maria "Betty" Tallchief worked hard to make her dreams come true. Maria Tallchief persisted, and—no matter what your dream is—you should too.

HOW YOU CAN PERSIST

by Christine Day

If you would like to help carry on Maria Tallchief's legacy, there are a lot of things you can do. Here are some ideas:

1. Dance with all your heart! Always remember Ruth's great advice.

2. Be respectful of other people's names. This includes legal first names and last

names, as well as the names people might choose for themselves.

3. Speak out against bullies.

4. Learn about the Native Americans in your own area. Who are they? What is their history? What are they up to right now? What can you do to honor them?

5. Visit tribally managed museums, cultural centers, or public powwows to celebrate and support the Native American community.

6. Attend a ballet performance, or another type of dance or stage production, to celebrate and support the arts.

7. Choreograph a dance routine with your friends.

8. Tell your friends and family the story
   of Maria Tallchief. Tell them about
   how she persisted even though she was
   bullied in school, and even though there
   weren't many American ballet stars
   who came before her.

Acknowledgments

....

To the Osage Nation Language Department: Thank you for reviewing the material in this book, and for adding Osage translations to each chapter title.

To Cynthia Leitich Smith (Muscogee Creek): Thank you for being an incredible friend, peer, and role model to me throughout my publishing journey. And thank you for recommending me for the She Persisted series. I hope that my work here will make you proud!

To Jill Santopolo and Talia Benamy: Thank you for welcoming me into the Persisterhood. Thank you for your great editorial feedback, as well as your delightfully exclamatory emails. It has been such a joy to work with you! I also need to express my gratitude to the rest of the Philomel team, as well as the copyeditors and fact-checkers, the marketing and publicity teams, the warehouse workers and delivery drivers, et al., associated with Penguin Random House. It takes a village to create a book and send it off into the world. I am thankful for everyone involved with this one.

To Suzie Townsend, Dani Segelbaum, and everyone else at New Leaf Literary: Thank you for supporting me through every book, every step of the way. Thank you for being patient with me whenever I have questions about the legal language in my contracts. Thank you for being the greatest and most reliable team an author could wish for.

To Alexandra Boiger and Gillian Flint: Thank you for capturing Maria's grace and radiance in your illustrations.

To Chelsea Clinton: Thank you for expanding *She Persisted* into a chapter book series. Your vision for these books is so inspiring. Thank you for uplifting these remarkable women and their accomplishments. Thank you for building a diverse group of woman writers and illustrators to share these stories with young readers. It has been an honor and a privilege to write Maria Tallchief's biography. I am so grateful to you.

To my former teachers, including: My third-grade teacher, Ms. Guthrie, who let me keep a book from her classroom library. My sixth-grade teacher, Ms. Willis, whose strict rules and high expectations inspired me to dream big and work hard. My eleventh-grade social studies teacher, Ms. Sukol, who genuinely cared about my well-being. My dance instructors at the Pacific Northwest Ballet School, who gave me a deep appreciation for the arts. And my many professors at the University of Washington, especially those from the Department of American Indian Studies.

To my family members, including: Mom and Dad—thank you for reading books with me every night in my childhood. Thank you for sitting me down at the table whenever you filled out your election ballots. You raised me to be a reader, an independent thinker, and an active participant in the democratic process, and I know you are still geeking out over the idea of your daughter sharing a book with President Clinton's daughter. I couldn't have made it here without you. Jenny, thank you for being my sister and my lifelong best friend. Mado and Elias, thank you for bringing the love of my life into the world, and for being such wonderful in-laws. Ever since you arrived in this country, you have worked so hard and given your family so much, and I'm grateful to know that my kids will grow up surrounded by your love. Christina and Josh, thank you for always making me laugh, and for making me an auntie.

To my husband, Mazen: I love you. So very much.

To my daughter, Mia: This book will come out sometime around your first birthday. I can't wait to share these words with you someday. I can't wait to bundle you up in my lap and point at this very page. And I hope you will feel my tremendous love for you as I say,

You are capable of anything.

⁓ *References* ⥱

"About." Dance Maker Academy.
www.dancemaker.net.

Anderson, Jack. "Maria Tallchief, a Dazzling
Ballerina and Muse for Balanchine, Dies at 88."
The New York Times, April 12, 2013.
www.nytimes.com/2013/04/13/arts/dance
/maria-tallchief-brilliant-ballerina-dies
-at-88.html.

Block, Gene D., and Mishuana R. Goeman. "Acknowledging Native Peoples at UCLA Events." UCLA: Office of the Chancellor, August 22, 2019. www.chancellor.ucla.edu /messages/acknowledging-native-peoples -ucla-events.

Curwen, Thomas. "Finding Tovaangar: Tongva, Los Angeles' first language, opens the door to a forgotten time and place." *Los Angeles Times*, May 9, 2019. www.latimes.com/projects/la-me -col1-tongva-language-native-american-tribe.

Greene, Sean, and Thomas Curwen. "Mapping the Tongva Villages of L.A.'s Past." *Los Angeles Times*, May 9, 2019. www.latimes .com/projects/la-me-tongva-map.

Halzack, Sarah. "Maria Tallchief, ballet star who was inspiration for Balanchine, dies at 88." *The Washington Post*, April 12, 2013. www.washingtonpost.com/local/obituaries /maria-tallchief-ballet-star-who-was-inspiration -for-balanchine-dies-at-88/2013/04/12 /5888f3de-c5dc-11df-94e1-c5afa35a9e59_story .html.

"Inside Wahzhazhe: The Story." Osage Ballet. www.osageballet.com/thestory.

"K-12 Lessons: Osage Ballet." The Osage Nation. www.osagenation-nsn.gov/k-12-lessons /k12-osage-ballet.

Kilian, Michael. "Maria Tallchief Back at
Center Stage as Kennedy Center Honoree."
Chicago Tribune, December 5, 1996.
www.chicagotribune.com/news
/ct-xpm-1996-12-05-9612050118-story.html.

Klein, Christopher. "The FBI's First Big Case:
The Osage Murders." History, August 31,
2018. www.history.com/news
/the-fbis-first-big-case-the-osage-murders.

Magill, Frank N. "Summary: Maria Tallchief."
*The 20th Century O-Z: Dictionary of
World Biography*. New York: Routledge,
Inc., 1999.

Norwood, Arlisha R. "Maria Tallchief."
National Women's History Museum, 2017.
www.womenshistory.org/education-resources
/biographies/maria-tallchief.

Tallchief, Maria, and Larry Kaplan. *Maria
Tallchief: America's Prima Ballerina.*
Gainesville: University Press of Florida,
2005.

"Thinking of Maria Tallchief on Her Birthday."
The National Museum of the American
Indian, January 24, 2016. www.blog.nmai
.si.edu/main/2016/01/maria-tallchief-on
-her-birthday.html.

Zotigh, Dennis. "Native Perspectives on the 40th Anniversary of the American Indian Religious Freedom Act." *Smithsonian Voices: National Museum of the American Indian,* November 30, 2018. www.smithsonianmag .com/blogs/national-museum-american-indian /2018/11/30/native-perspectives-american -indian-religious-freedom-act.

CHRISTINE DAY (Upper Skagit) grew up in Seattle, nestled between the sea, the mountains, and the pages of her favorite books. Her debut novel, *I Can Make This Promise*, was a best book of the year from *Kirkus Reviews*, *School Library Journal*, NPR, and the Chicago Public Library, as well as a Charlotte Huck Award Honor Book and an American Indian Youth Literature Award Honor Book. Her second novel is titled *The Sea in Winter*. Christine lives in the Pacific Northwest with her family.

Photo credit: Jessica Wood

You can visit Christine Day online at
bychristineday.com
or follow her on Twitter and Instagram
@bychristineday

GILLIAN FLINT has worked as a professional illustrator since earning an animation and illustration degree in 2003. Her work has since been published in the UK, USA and Australia. In her spare time, Gillian enjoys reading, spending time with her family and puttering about in the garden on sunny days. She lives in the northwest of England.

You can visit Gillian Flint online at
gillianflint.com
or follow her on Twitter
@GillianFlint
and on Instagram
@gillianflint_illustration

CHELSEA CLINTON is the author of the #1 *New York Times* bestseller *She Persisted: 13 American Women Who Changed the World*; *She Persisted Around the World: 13 Women Who Changed History*; *She Persisted in Sports: American Olympians Who Changed the Game*; *Don't Let Them Disappear: 12 Endangered Species Across the Globe*; *It's Your World: Get Informed, Get Inspired & Get Going!*; *Start Now!: You Can Make a Difference*; with Hillary Clinton, *Grandma's Gardens* and *Gutsy Women*; and, with Devi Sridhar, *Governing Global Health: Who Runs the World and Why?* She is also the Vice Chair of the Clinton Foundation, where she works on many initiatives, including those that help empower the next generation of leaders. She lives in New York City with her husband, Marc, their children and their dog, Soren.

You can follow Chelsea Clinton on Twitter
@ChelseaClinton
or on Facebook at
facebook.com/chelseaclinton

ALEXANDRA BOIGER has illustrated nearly twenty picture books, including the She Persisted books by Chelsea Clinton; the popular Tallulah series by Marilyn Singer; and the Max and Marla books, which she also wrote. Originally from Munich, Germany, she now lives outside of San Francisco, California, with her husband, Andrea, daughter, Vanessa, and two cats, Luiso and Winter.

Photo credit: *Vanessa Blasich*

You can visit Alexandra Boiger online at
alexandraboiger.com
or follow her on Instagram
@alexandra_boiger

Don't miss the rest of the books in the

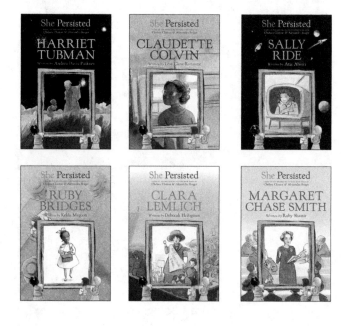

She Persisted series!

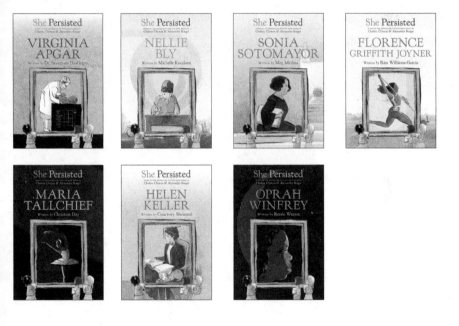